Katrina,
The Mystery of Prayer

Katrina,
The Mystery of Prayer

Penny Castleman-Johansen

XULON ELITE

Xulon Press Elite
2301 Lucien Way #415
Maitland, FL 32751
407.339.4217
www.xulonpress.com

© 2023 by Penny Castleman-Johansen

All rights reserved solely by the author. The author guarantees all contents are original and do not infringe upon the legal rights of any other person or work. No part of this book may be reproduced in any form without the permission of the author.

Due to the changing nature of the Internet, if there are any web addresses, links, or URLs included in this manuscript, these may have been altered and may no longer be accessible. The views and opinions shared in this book belong solely to the author and do not necessarily reflect those of the publisher. The publisher therefore disclaims responsibility for the views or opinions expressed within the work.

Unless otherwise indicated, SScripture quotations taken from the New King James Version (NKJV). Copyright © 1982 by Thomas Nelson, Inc. Used by permission. All rights reserved.

Paperback ISBN-13: 978-1-66288-090-2
Ebook ISBN-13: 978-1-66288-091-9

Let me introduce myself: I am Penny Castleman-Johansen. I am a Bible-believing, God-fearing, Christian wife, mother, grandmother, paramedic, and author. One fun fact about me: I went out for the summer and drove a tractor-trailer, and have driven a school bus before going into EMS. I enjoy reading, cooking, and spending time with my family. I love kids and have a heart for the youth. I am a member of Water Valley Pentecostal Tabernacle. Most importantly, Jesus is awesome. I cannot say enough of what He has done for me in my life. My prayer for this book is that whoever reads it knows that God loves you enough to give you His Son, and that Jesus loves you enough to die for you. The price has been paid. No matter what you have done or where you have been, you are forgiven when you accept Him as your Lord and Savior. Just call His name.

Dedicated to these people:

I want to dedicate this book to my Heavenly Father and my Savior, Jesus. I also want to recognize my husband of 32 years, Keith Johansen. When I feel weak and need encouragement, he always knows what verse to give me. My kids, Joshua (Sarah), Tomi (Keith), and Paige, who had to listen to me for years while getting the courage to complete this task. My grandchildren, Degan Case, Jasper, Laela, Isabella, Jackson, and Peyton: I love all of you, to the moon and beyond. My best friend and prayer partner, Jenny Whichard, you have always been there when I felt like quitting. My friend, coworker, and Brother in Christ, Logan Campbell, thank you for proofreading and encouraging me. Brother Charles and Sister Sarah Mitchell for pushing me to publish this. Thank you, Brother Markus, and Sister Emily McClure for following the calling and ministering with love. I want to recognize the Christian Heritage Worship Center and the ones who ministered to the youth there. Never give up and know that all of you have affected more lives than just the youth. Below is a picture of camp 2022: "Let's Go!" I want each person who was there to know this book is dedicated to all of you.

Youth Camp 2022, "Let's Go!"

My Grandkids
Front Row- Jasper, Laela, Case
Back Row- Bella, Jackson, & Peyton

McClure Family

Front Row- Mavis
Second Row – Lucy
Back Row- Naomi, Markus, Emily, & Adah

Devan & Adrianna Cole

Contents

Chapter 1 1
Chapter 2 5
Chapter 3 7
Chapter 4 13
Chapter 5 17
Chapter 6 21
Chapter 7 25
Chapter 8 29
Chapter 9 33
Chapter 10 43
Chapter 11 47
Chapter 12 53
Chapter 13 59
Chapter 14 65
Chapter 15 71

Chapter 1

What is that? It sounds so eerie. "Is someone there?" Katrina asks. "Come on, who is out there?"

The sound is growing, but no one answers. She can see out across the lake. There is not a breeze though. All of a sudden, the window blows open and her kid brother, Jarod, jumps inside.

"What is wrong with you? You scared me. Mom and Dad will hear about this when they get home," Katrina says.

"Go ahead. I'll tell them about the books you have been reading," Jarod says to her.

"Okay, so I scared myself, with a lot of help from you. Mom always wants us to read Christian books, but they are *always* the same. Just once, I would like to see a Christian action-adventure book," Katrina says.

"Yeah, I know what you mean. She talks about spiritual warfare, but that's all talk. Everybody knows it is old fashioned."

"Katrina and Jarod, we're home," Dad calls.

"Let's see what they got us," replies Katrina.

Little do the kids know that their adventure has just started. An angel stands outside the window, in the shadows, longing to help them, but knows he cannot.

"Hey, we got you some books today!" Mom says.

Katrina, The Mystery of Prayer

"Let's see them," says Jarod, reaching out his hand. "Oh no, not another book on prayer."

"Yes, another book on prayer. I want you to understand its importance. I know you feel I am old-fashioned, but prayer is not old-fashioned. We have freedom to worship Jesus while others do not. There is *power* in prayer. That power comes from God; there is no other power. Just promise me you will read them," says Mom.

"Okay, we promise," they mumble soberly.

"Please do not make light of this," states Mom.

"Well, let's get some sleep," Dad says.

Mom and Dad leave the kids and head off to bed, wondering as they walk to their room if the kids realize how much Jesus loves them, but not saying a word to the other one.

"Boy, do you really believe Mom? She thinks prayer is the answer to everything," says Katrina.

"Yeah, I know, but what if she is right?" asks Jarod.

"Oh, you can't be serious. It is all talk. There is nothing to it," Katrina replies.

"Yeah, but what if?" questions Jarod.

"Go to bed," Katrina says, sounding tired. "Goodnight."

Jarod heads to his room, wondering who is right, Mom and Dad, or Katrina.

"Dale, I do not think the kids really understand. I pray they never have to deal with some of the things we dealt with in our younger years."

"They'll be okay; just give them time and they will be alright," Dale says, as he falls asleep.

Chapter 1

Peggy begins to pray. "Lord, please lead my children to You and do whatever it takes for them to realize who You are, and Your love, grace, and goodness. In Jesus's name, Amen!"

Peggy does not realize what she is asking while the angel is watching over her as she goes to sleep. The angel is looking at her soberly, knowing what is about to take place, and asks God to strengthen them all.

Chapter 2

"**Wake up! What** is that smell?" Peggy asks. "Oh no, the smoke alarms didn't go off! Dale, we have to get the kids out!"

"I'll get them. You meet us outside," replies Dale.

As Dale goes in to get the kids, there is total darkness from the fire in the attic. Dale hurries, gets both kids to a window, and helps them out to the yard. Peggy feels her way to the stairs. As she is going down the stairs, they collapse. Darkness surrounds her.

Dale, Jarod, and Katrina are waiting for Peggy outside the house. Someone passing by calls the fire department and ambulance. "Oh God, where is Mom?" Katrina is crying.

"I am sure she is okay," Dale says. Knowing someone has to stay with the kids.

People are coming from all over town. The firefighters rush into the house and pull something out of it. It cannot be Mom. She knows to crawl out, but why is he pulling furniture? Someone yells, "She is alive!"

Dale and the kids run as fast as they can to get to her, but it is too late. They have closed the ambulance doors. The house is bright orange from the fire, with nothing left but flames. Firefighters are spraying water,

Katrina, The Mystery of Prayer

except one. He is walking slowly to the family, with a face of distress.

"They are taking her to New Hope Memorial Hospital," the fireman says. "I hope she pulls through this. She is not burned, but smoke kills more times than fire, Dale."

Brother Mike approaches as the firemen are leaving. He is the pastor of their church. "Let me take the kids to my house. You go to the hospital. We will start a prayer line immediately. Peggy is a strong Christian woman. Just trust the Lord."

"Okay, Brother Mike, take the kids. Peggy needs me," Dale cries.

"Katrina and Jarod, go with Brother Mike. I will be there as soon as I know how your mom is doing."

The kids shout, "But, Dad!"

"No 'buts.' Do this please and pray. That is all your mother would ask of you. I love you and so does she. We have to have faith."

"Okay," they both agree.

The ambulance is rushing to the hospital when the EMT driving hears. "We are losing her," says the paramedic. "Start CPR."

As the ambulance pulls into the emergency room, they get a heartbeat. "Hurry, we resuscitated her. Her pulse is weak, but we have one."

Chapter 3

The family and their pastor go visit Peggy in the hospital. She is still in a coma after three days, but she is alive.

"Mom, please wake up," Katrina cries.

"Katrina, calm down, you know she would wake up if she could. She is in Jesus's hands now." Says Dad.

"That is all you talk about: Jesus. What about us? I am so tired of hearing about Him. If He really cares, Mom would not be in this coma!" shouts Katrina.

"You know better than that," Dad says.

"No, I don't. Just leave me alone," Katrina says, as she storms out of the room.

"Peggy, I know why you were so worried now. Katrina was okay as long as you were praying over her, but now I am worried. I can't do this alone. Please come back to us soon," sobs Dale.

Jarod and Katrina stand outside in the hall crying, as Brother Mike tries to console them. "Kids, I know this must be hard, but God is with her. Let's pray for her and you."

"You do not know, and it is *all* lies. If God really cares, He would help her wake up right now. He is a fake," Katrina yells.

Katrina, The Mystery of Prayer

"Katrina, we never see the big picture, only God does. What we want may not be His plan. When we pray, we petition Him with our request. Did your mom give you everything you wanted, just because you asked for it? No! Do you know why? She knew more than you."

Jarod asks, "Is that why she made us promise to read the books on prayer?"

"Yes," says Brother Mike.

"They burned up in the house, along with everything else," Jarod cries.

"When we leave here, we will go by the bookstore and see if Mr. Johnson has those books, she gave you. Do you remember what they were?"

"I remember the cover," Jarod replies.

"Good enough. Dale, we were just about to pray. Would you join us?" asks Brother Mike as Dale walks out of the room to join them.

"Dear Heavenly Father, help Peggy," Brother Mike says. "You know what the need is even before we ask and be with her family. They need her so badly. We know Your Will is going to be done and that is all we really want from You. Send comfort for the hurt that the kids are feeling. Lord, Katrina needs You right now. She is feeling lost without her mother. Show her Your way. Lord, be with Jarod as he struggles with this situation. Let him know Your strength and endurance. Lord, also be with Dale. Dale is the head of the house. You put him there, with Peggy as a helpmate. Now he has to do it alone; guide him as he leads this family. Lord, we thank you for everything You do in our lives

Chapter 3

and what You are doing now. We love You, in Jesus's name, Amen."

Brother Mike starts walking out to go to the bookstore with the kids. Dale goes back into the room to see Peggy. The nurse comes in about the same time to check on her vitals. "Everything seems to be okay," says the nurse.

"How long will she be like this?" Dale asks.

"We don't know; sometimes days, other times they never wake up," says the nurse.

"I believe she will wake up. God has never let me down," Dale replies, in all earnestness.

"That is what my grandmother used to say too. I never seemed to have her faith though."

"Peggy always said, 'Just trust Him and it will work out. Maybe not the way we want it to, but in His way," Dale says soberly. "Maybe I needed her prayers. I sure wish my daughter felt that way. Have you? Well, I never really ask people, but are you saved?"

"I like to think so. I help people, and I am a good person," the nurse replies.

"No, I mean have you accepted Him into your heart?"

"I walked the aisle, but I am still the same."

"When you say, 'the same,' do you mean spiritually or physically?"

"I don't feel any different on the inside. Every day is like any other; nothing really changed."

"That is a scary thought. I never want to be only 'the same.' Even Levi was not the same after accepting Christ," replies Dale.

"So, do you believe God has a reason for everything? Even if it looks bad?"

9

Katrina, The Mystery of Prayer

"Sure, so many times we think all about our lives, but really it is all about Him. Sometimes, it takes something big to get our attention," Dale says. "If you ever need a friend call and if you ever want to visit our church, the doors are always open."

"What church do you go to?" asks the nurse.

"Johnson Baptist Church; it is a Bible-believing church. The pastor preaches straight out of the Bible. Sometimes, it seems like he is talking only to me. That can be scary at times, but it always helps keep me on the right path."

"What do you mean by 'path?'"

"Well, even Christians mess up, but we strive to be Christ-like. Just because we are saved by grace, it doesn't give us the right to sin because we can."

Sue, Peggy's best friend, walks into the room to visit, while Dale is talking with the nurse. She does not realize he is having an important conversation about the Lord.

"Hi, Dale."

"Oh, hi, Sue," replies Dale.

Since there is someone else in the room, the nurse politely excuses herself.

"What is wrong with her?" asks Sue.

"Sue, she needs our prayers, and so does Peggy. I know the Holy Spirit is doing something. I only wish I could understand all of this."

"Let's put her on the prayer chain at church," states Sue.

"Well, that may be hard to do. I didn't ask her what her name was," Dale says soberly.

Chapter 3

Sue begins to laugh and says, "God has to be doing something. You talked to a complete stranger about Him, and you don't even know her name. That sounds more like Peggy than you."

"Yeah, I know. Okay, I will ask her name when I leave," Dale says.

Chapter 4

"**Oh, God, why** can't I open my eyes or move? It's not like I can't hear Katrina crying or Dale talking. He is even holding my hand. Please, God, help me!" Peggy cries.

"Peace, Peggy," says the angel from God.

"Who are you?" asks Peggy.

"I am an angel from God, sent just for you."

"I want to wake up!" Peggy cries.

"God knows, but He needs you here right now."

"I really need to help my family right now," says Peggy.

"You *are* helping them," the angel states.

"How?"

"By being here. God has work for you. Your job right now is to be *here*. Sometimes, your job is to stand still. Would you really do that if you were not in a coma?"

"Well, I *know* God knows what is best, but I still have a job to do, or He would have taken me home."

"Yes, but it is not time. You will have years to help people. Keep looking to Jesus," says the angel.

"Dale, Is Peggy crying?" asks Sue.

"No. The doctors say her tear ducts are overacting," replies Dale.

Katrina, The Mystery of Prayer

"I don't know; doctors can be wrong. They don't even know why she has not woken up yet."

"How are Chuck and the kids?" Dale asks, trying to change the subject.

"Nice move, changing the subject. They are fine. Have you decided what you and the kids are going to do?"

"No, I need to start looking for a new place. We can't stay at Brother Mike's forever."

"There is a house for sale near ours if you thought about buying a new place. I can help with the kids. Toni and Rick would love it," says Sue.

"I may check it out. Peggy always took care of the moving, and of the kids. I never realized how much she sacrificed," Dale says, and starts to cry.

"Does he know it was never a sacrifice? I did it because I love them," cries Peggy to the angel.

"He will when God wants him to know."

"Is this why I am here?" asks Peggy.

"Only God Himself knows that." Says the angel.

"Father, Your will be done. Send angels to do Your mighty work, in Jesus's name," prays Peggy.

"Amen. Rest now in His Love," The angel says.

Dale waits by Peggy's side. "I know it is time to go, but maybe she will wake up. God, help me," cries Dale.

Dale thinks, *I have such a strong need to check on the kids. Maybe it is time to find a new house for the family.*

Dale looks around as he is leaving but does not see the nurse. So, he says a prayer for her instead. "Lord, you know the nurse, even if I don't know her name. It feels like she is struggling; help her to find a relationship with you. In Jesus's name, Amen."

Chapter 4

As weeks go by, Peggy still lays in the coma. Dale and the kids move into a new house, and their visits become less frequent.

"Why don't they come? I feel so lonely," cries Peggy.

"We have had this discussion: God's will," answers the angel.

"I know, and I love Him with all my heart."

Chapter 5

"**Dad, can I** go out this weekend?" Katrina asks. "It's not a date or anything. We will be at Gina's house with some friends."

"Are any of these friends' boys?" asks Dad.

"Oh, come on, Dad."

"You know the rules. No dating until you are sixteen."

"I know, but it is not a date," pouts Katrina.

"The answer is no, and don't you have a youth meeting this Friday?" he asks.

"Sure, but we do that all the time."

"Yeah, and if you would pay attention, maybe you would enjoy it," says Jarod. "We discussed the books Mom had us read. It helped Dad."

"Not for me," cries Katrina.

"Katrina is there anything I can do to help you deal with our situation?" asks Dad.

"It is always 'our situation,' and never 'my situation!'" yells Katrina.

"Katrina enough, I said no to going out, so get over it!" yells her dad. Frustration is hitting him hard.

Katrina cries, running from the room, because she has not gotten her way. *Life has become hard, and no one understands how I feel*, she thinks.

"Jarod, what am I doing wrong?" Dale asks his son.

Katrina, The Mystery of Prayer

"Dad, I am eleven. How should I know?" asks Jarod. "But she never gave Mom's books a chance. It helped me, and I feel closer to the Lord."

"I feel closer too, but Katrina seems farther," says Dale, sighing.

"She never *was* close, Dad. On the night of the fire, she was reading a book that you and mom would not let her read: It scared her."

"That is what your mom was worried about that night," explains Dad.

"Can we go see Mom? I haven't been there lately," asks Jarod.

"Yes, let's go tomorrow. I have a meeting tonight with the Chief of Police, Tom Smith."

Tomorrow never comes because the insurance company has contacted the hospital. Peggy is being moved to a nursing home. They feel she is a lost cause. The nearest one is right out of town. Dale goes to the nursing home to do the paperwork for Peggy. He wonders, *how am I going to tell the kids, and how are they going to take it?*

Dale prays: "God, it has been so much on them, and now they won't be able to see her as often. Katrina is having such a problem with authority. Jarod is still searching for answers. I am not even sure what I am doing sometimes. God, when are You going to bring her back to me? I need her so badly it hurts. Help me! No, help *us*. Thank you, God, for Your mercy and grace, through Your Son, Jesus."

Friday night comes, and Katrina does not let up: she sulks and pouts all weekend, to no avail.

Chapter 5

"Why can't I go?" she repeats. "*Everybody* will be there. Are you trying to make me a nun or something?"

"The answer is no, and that is all I am saying on this subject!" replies Dad.

As Katrina walks out of the room, she mumbles to herself, "We will see about that, Dad."

Katrina calls Gina as soon as she reaches her room. "Gina, you won't believe how old-fashioned my dad is about dating."

"No, I *can't* believe it. I'm allowed to do what I want to do, but at least you know he is there for you," states Gina.

"Yeah, I know, but the control can be unbearable. Sometimes, I wish he was not there so much. I mean, you can date. It is a closed subject here," whines Katrina.

"So, your dad said no?" asks Gina.

"Right. But he is asleep by 9:30 or 10:00 p.m. I'll be over then. The party won't really get started until midnight. I will be there, don't worry. We better get off the phone before someone picks up and hears us. See you soon."

"Bye, Katrina."

"Jarod, what time do I need to pick you up at church?" Dad asks.

"Well, Rick wants to know if I can spend the night," hints Jarod.

"Is it okay with his mother?"

"Yeah, we just have to clear it with you," replies Jarod.

"It is cleared."

"Thanks, Dad!"

19

Chapter 6

Dale decides to go visit Peggy at the nursing home. The leaves are changing on the trees, as quickly as the kids are changing each day. You can feel fall in the air already. It seems so peaceful, but he knows how that can change in a second.

"Hi, how is Peggy doing?" Dale asks the nurse.

"She is doing the same today. The doctor came by; he still has no clue what is going on though. She can breathe on her own, but there is no brain activity, according to him."

"Only God knows what is going on inside of her," Dale says. "I only wish He would let me in on the information though."

"That is the truth," replies the nurse.

"I will speak to you later," says Dale.

He walks into Peggy's room; it makes him want to cry seeing her lying in the bed so peacefully. *If you only knew*, he thinks.

"Peggy, I love you. I keep praying you can hear me and will wake up. The kids are doing fine, physically. Jarod is praying all the time, like you did at home. Katrina worries me though; she wants to go to a party at a girl's house tonight. Her name is Gina something. I told her no. I wish you were here to help. She wants

Katrina, The Mystery of Prayer

to start dating at fourteen. I am realizing why you had to be with them and give them guidance. Things have changed since you and I dated. I know you can't hear me, but it helps to talk to you about the kids."

Peggy lies there, with no response. Dale starts praying for her, and their family: "God, please keep your hand on Peggy and the kids; they mean so much to me. Forgive me where I have fallen short. Give me Your strength; I could never do this alone. Jesus, thank you for loving me; I know I am asking for so much from you lately. Forgive me and help me, in Jesus's precious name. Amen."

"Peggy, I have to go now. I love you," Dale says, as he walks out of the door crying.

Peggy lays there, not able to move or speak out loud, but cries within, "God, I know you have a purpose. How can I help lying here? Dale is hurting so badly. Jarod seems to be okay, but Katrina, she is another subject all together. That party is not a good sign. Gina needs prayer. Her parties in the past have been, well, kind of wild. Thank goodness Dale said no."

"Peggy, God's plan is in motion, as I speak with you," says the angel.

"How?"

"Dale said he is asking more of God lately, right?"

"Well, yes," replies Peggy.

"He would not be doing that if you were there right now. Jarod is reaching out more too."

"You have not said a thing about Katrina. Why?" Peggy asks, as a tear falls off her cheek.

"She is harder to reach right now. She hasn't asked Jesus into her heart yet. She lets everyone

Chapter 6

see what she thinks they want but she has not given herself to Him. Give God time and keep praying and praising Him."

Chapter 7

Katrina goes upstairs and gets ready for the party, instead of bed. "I am not sure what top to wear with these jeans. Yeah, I will wear the red top. It shows some cleavage, but not too much. It will show off my figure. I can do my makeup at Gina's house. Dad will never know I have gone out. I can slip out after he goes to sleep," Katrina says quietly to herself.

Jarod and Dale have already discussed Katrina; they both know she has given up too easily. They are not sure what she is about to do, but she did not go to the youth meeting, and stayed home instead of going to see her mother. She has not missed seeing her mother since the accident.

"Katrina, I am home," calls Dale.

"Dad, I'm up here," yells Katrina from upstairs. "I'm not feeling good. I think all I need is some sleep. I'll see you in the morning."

"Alright, goodnight."

"Goodnight, Daddy," Katrina says so sweetly.

She sure is playing it up, Dale thinks. *I really have to keep my eyes and ears open tonight. Katrina is up to something.*

Two hours go by, and Katrina thinks her dad is asleep. She slowly opens her window, and crawls onto

Katrina, The Mystery of Prayer

the roof. She has placed the ladder at the back corner of the house. She slowly climbs down. It's dark, but she can deal with it tonight.

She is going to meet Eric at the party. Eric is so cute, with those big brown eyes and blonde hair. She thinks they look so good together. She wonders why it seems so creepy tonight. There isn't even a breeze. It is like being shut up inside, but she is outside. Mom would tell her to pray, but she would have known what I was doing tonight. If Daddy really cares, he would listen to me, but he doesn't. Just up the street is Gina's house, and boy it is lit up. Katrina does not realize there are so many people coming. She can hear the music from here. Cool, it is Bon Jovi!

"Gina, hey girl, I did not know there would be so many people," Katrina yells, as she sees Gina.

"Yeah, I invited some people from the college. Look at that cute guy! Isn't he gorgeous? I also saw Eric around here and he was looking for you," Gina says, with a grin.

"Well, here I am, so let's go find him! What is that smell?" Katrina asks, as she wrinkles her nose.

"It is just someone doing pot or meth; it is so cool. There is anything you want to drink but be careful. I don't know some of these guys. Rumor has it they use the date rape drug. You should be okay if you are with Eric."

"There's Eric now; let's go, Gina."

"No way; he is your guy. I am going to find my own," Gina yells, as she walks away.

Chapter 7

"Katrina, I have been looking for you everywhere. I thought you might have changed your mind and followed the rules," states Eric, smiling.

"I told you I would be here, and here I am. I make my own decisions."

"Yeah, right, I hear you. Here, I got you a drink," Eric says.

"Thanks," replies Katrina, grabbing the drink.

"Have you thought about what we talked about yesterday?"

"Yeah, but I'm still not ready to have sex. I know most of our friends are, but I guess some of the old-fashioned stuff rubbed off on me. Who knew?"

"Katrina, it really is not a big deal, I brought protection."

"Eric, you said you would respect my answer."

"Okay, I'll let it go, even though I do love you and want to show you how much," Eric says, with sincere conviction.

"I love you too, but the answer is still No! Let's go dance," Katrina says.

Eric thinks he will have Katrina tonight and thank God for those college boys and their wonder drug. But, God didn't have anything to do with it.

Chapter 8

Dale is at home, sound asleep when all of a sudden, he thinks he hears Katrina. "Katrina, is that you? Are you okay?"

No answer comes. He wonders if she can hear him. He walks to the door and knocks. He can hear her radio. He opens the door and realizes something is wrong. Katrina's bed is still made up. Dale thinks, *I knew I should have set my alarm and checked on her sooner.* Things seemed so dark, as Dale goes downstairs and calls the police.

"Katrina are you having a good time?" asks Eric.

"Yea, but I feel sleepy," Katrina replies.

"Let's go up to Gina's room and lay down for a bit. Maybe you will feel better soon. I promise I won't touch you unless you want me to."

"Okay, maybe that will help," Katrina says wearily, as she leans on Eric.

A few of the college boys see them going upstairs and laugh. "Let the good times roll!"

"Don't you mean a roll in the hay?" another one responds.

"Yeah, she will never know what hit her. Let's go find some girls to roll in the hay with too!"

Katrina, The Mystery of Prayer

Back home, Katrina's dad is talking to the police. "Hi Tom, this is Dale Casteel. I have a problem. I hope you can help me tonight. Katrina has taken off to some party. I don't know where. I know the girl's name is Gina. Do you have any news about a party?"

"Yes, there have been a few complaints about the noise and kids at a house on Meadow Street."

"Can you give me the address?" asks Dad.

"Not really, but I can do one better. Let me take a deputy over there and check it out for you. You need to be at home in case she comes home. Sometimes, those parties get wild. So, start praying for her right now. I'll speak to you soon."

Back at the party. Eric asks, "Katrina, does that feel good?"

"Yeah, I am feeling relaxed now, but I can't seem to sit up. Does it feel hot in here?" Katrina says softly.

"Maybe a little bit. Loosen your top buttons and let me rub your shoulders. How does that feel?"

Katrina is getting concerned with how she is feeling, and asks, "Eric, why do I feel so weird?"

"I don't know, Katrina." Eric replies, realizing he can do anything he wants, and Katrina can't do anything about it. The other boys said she would not remember anything. Yet, something is telling him not to touch her, but no one will know. He slowly tries to take her shirt off.

"What do you think you are doing?" Katrina whispers.

"Katrina, I thought you would feel better if I took your shirt off."

"No!"

30

Chapter 8

He ignores her and keeps going. Katrina is wondering why she cannot fight him. "Please, somebody help me! I can't let him rape me. I know that is what is going to happen. Why didn't I listen?"

Just as Eric gets her shirt off, the door opens.

"What do you think you are doing?" asks Tom, the chief of police.

Eric does not even look up to see who it is at the door. "Get out and find yourself another room. This one is taken," replies Eric.

Chief Tom sees the scared look on Katrina's face. He wonders why she isn't fighting him. That is not like her. She normally would fight like a wildcat. She never let people walk all over her. "What is your name? Katrina are you okay?" asks the Chief.

Eric turns around and realizes who is standing at the door.

"I can't seem to move," she slurs.

"What have you given her, and I asked your name!" yells the Chief.

"My name is Eric, and that is all I am saying to you."

"Good idea. I have a feeling you are going to need a good lawyer."

Chief Tom turns back to Katrina and asks, "Katrina, listen to me, did he give you anything? Pills, cigarettes, or a drink?"

"Yes, the glass is on the table over there," she says slowly.

"Katrina, I need you to listen carefully, okay? I need you to stay awake. I believe the boy laced your drink with a drug. I am calling 911. Hold on, okay?"

Katrina, The Mystery of Prayer

Chief Tom gets on his radio, "Yes, I need an ambulance at 1429 Meadow Wood Avenue. I have a 14-year-old female, who seems to be drugged. She can talk but is unable to move."

911 operator replies, "We will have a unit there as soon as we can."

"Thank you!"

"Katrina, they are on their way, just hold on," says Chief Tom.

Chief Tom turns toward Eric and says, "Eric, you have some questions to answer."

"Deputy Paul, please take him to the station."

"Yes, sir, this way, Eric. I hope for your sake this is not what it looks like."

Chief Tom looks around the house and yells, "Everybody out, unless you want to be arrested. This party is over."

Chapter 9

"**Hi Dale, it** is Tom. I found Katrina. She seems to have been drugged, but we got there before her boyfriend could touch her."

"Can I talk to her?" asks Dale.

"No, she is being taken to New Hope Memorial Hospital. They need to check her out to make sure she is okay. She can talk, but her speech is slurred, and she can't move."

"She can't move? What?" Dale cries out.

"Dale, listen, call Brother Mike to get a prayer chain going, and get to the hospital. She is scared and has every right to be."

Katrina lays on the bed thinking about everything: *Why did he do this? Is this what Mom feels like? It is so scary and lonely. I can hear everything, but they don't even realize it. Why did I say those things in front of Mom? If I survive this, I am going to see Mom.*

Katrina could not see the angels around her. "She still hasn't asked Jesus into her heart," an angel of the Lord says sadly.

"I know. She is getting closer, but is not there yet. She may let things get worse before she sees that Jesus is the answer," the angel says, shaking his head sadly.

"Katrina are you still awake?" asks Chief Tom.

Katrina, The Mystery of Prayer

"Yes, but I am sleepy."

"Stay with me. The paramedics will be here soon."

As he is speaking, the door opens, and the paramedics race into the room. "How are her vitals?"

"I don't know. She can't move and she is sleepy. Her speech is slurred. A boy gave her a drink. The glass is on the table," says Chief Tom.

"We will check her out, and you have the glass to check out, but I can almost guarantee what is wrong with her. It will wear off in about eight hours and she will have a headache. She won't be able to remember most of this."

"She could have been hurt really bad if her father had not called." Says Chief Tom.

"She is one of the lucky ones," replies the paramedic.

"No, she is blessed because of prayer," answers Chief Tom.

The ambulance rushes her to the hospital. Dale and Brother Mike race to meet them at the hospital. *The night seems quiet and eerie, just like when Peggy went into her coma,* thinks Dale.

"God, please help Katrina! She needs you so much right now. She may not know You, or she may be going astray. I don't know what to do. Please help her and me," Dale prays.

They all reach the hospital about the same time. "Katrina, can you hear me?" calls her dad, as he finds and enters the room.

She cannot respond with her voice. All she can think about is needing help. Why, Daddy, aren't you helping me? You always let me down, but Mom never did. Mommy, please come to me. I need you!" she thinks.

Chapter 9

Katrina still cannot see the angels around her. She is blinded until she accepts Jesus.

"Baby, Daddy is here. Why is she not moving? Is she okay?" Dale pleads with the nurse.

"Sir, please wait outside while we examine her."

"No, I will not go out so you can examine her. She is my daughter, a minor, and as her father, I will stay."

"Okay, but will you please have a seat?" asks the nurse.

The nurse takes her vitals, and the lab takes the drink to examine it. It is indeed drugged. Katrina sleeps the night through. There will be no memory of tonight's events.

"Mr. Casteel, can we talk outside please?" asks the doctor.

"Yes."

"She is very lucky. We will be keeping her overnight. She was drugged, but there are no signs of rape. I don't know who or what protected her, but something did. Most girls aren't so lucky."

"Luck had nothing to do with it. God did," replies Dale.

"She will have no memory of tonight's events," the doctor says.

"I understand," Dale says, with uncertainty.

The doctor leaves the room and gives them some privacy. Katrina looks like an angel sleeping there. *Where did all the time go?* Dale thinks.

"God, it is me again. It seems I am always calling on You lately. Thank you for keeping my baby safe. Katrina needs You now more than ever. She is so weak. She thinks she can do anything, but we know the truth.

Katrina, The Mystery of Prayer

Please, help her to accept You. Do whatever it takes to get her attention. I pray this, in Your Precious Son's name, Jesus. Amen."

No one can see the angels watching over her. "Dale, God heard your prayer. He will do whatever it takes. I hope you are ready," replies the angel.

Sunlight is coming through the hospital window. Katrina turns and watches her dad as he sleeps. She begins to wonder why they are at the hospital. She knows her head hurts, but that is no reason to be in the hospital. Nothing seems to be broken. Her dad looks so tired, even sleeping. She remembers when he looked so much younger. Mom was the reason. Now he looks old. Why did things have to change?

"Daddy!" calls Katrina. "Are you awake?"

"Katrina, I am now," Dale answers, eyes opening wide, as he quickly sits up. "Thank God, you are okay. Do you hurt anywhere? How does your head feel?"

"My head is hurting a little. Why are we here?"

"What do you remember about last night?" asks her dad.

"Not much. I got ready and then... oh, no! You know I snuck out of the house."

"Yes, I do," her father says, sighing.

"Why are you yelling at me?" wails Katrina.

Dale ignores Katrina's question. The doctor had said she would have sensitivity to sound for a day or so.

"I am glad you are safe," he says. "Now let's finish talking about what you remember from last night," he reaches for her hand.

"I went to Gina's. I met up with Eric, and then I started feeling really weird. So, he took me to Gina's

Chapter 9

room to lie down. Everything after that is a blur," says Katrina.

"Katrina, Eric drugged you."

"What? No! He loves me!" yells Katrina to her dad.

"Honey, I realize this is hard, but he did, and he was arrested. I believe for rape or attempted rape. I am not sure what the charges are."

"Who did he rape?" asks Katrina.

"I said attempted to rape. It was you."

"Dad," replies Katrina, "I would have remembered something like that."

"No, Katrina, you would not have known it. He drugged your drink."

"I don't believe you. You just don't want me to see him or Gina anymore. I don't know how you set this up," Katrina cries. "My head hurts, please leave me alone," she says, changing the subject.

Dale can see it is no use talking to his daughter. *No matter what I say, it will be wrong,* he thinks.

"Please, God, send me a sign."

Police Chief Tom walks in and asks, "How is she today?"

"Ask *her*; she is not speaking to me... again," Dale says.

"Katrina, are you okay?"

"Yeah, but what I have been told is unbelievable," Katrina says.

"Dale, I told you I needed to speak to her first. You may have hurt the case," Chief Tom scolds.

"What case?" asks Katrina.

"One thing at a time. Let's talk, Katrina," replies Chief Tom.

Katrina, The Mystery of Prayer

"Okay, talk."

"What do you remember?" He asks.

"I already told my dad. I went to the party, met up with my boyfriend, and we went upstairs. What is the big deal?"

"Well, underage drinking, drugs, and no supervision," he replies.

"Yeah, but I am innocent. Am I being arrested or something?" asks Katrina.

"No, but some others may be before long."

"What do you mean before long?"

"We did not have enough evidence to arrest him," says the chief.

"Stop it if you are talking about Eric. He would never hurt me; he loves me!" yells Katrina.

The nurse walks in and yells, "Enough. We have to look after our patient. Please, step outside to argue."

"Thank you," cries Katrina.

Both men walk out the door as the nurse, Sandra, says, "Anytime, honey. Now, let's check your vitals."

"Okay, can you tell me why I am here?" asks Katrina.

"I know they brought you in last night. They said you looked like your mother, and it is true," replies the nurse.

"Do you know my mom?" asks Katrina shyly.

"No, I took care of her. How is she now?"

"The same as usual. People seem to forget about her, even me, sometimes."

"Not me. She was one of the best things that happened to me. I wish it had been under better terms," Sandra replies sadly.

"What are you talking about?"

38

Chapter 9

"Can I call you Katrina? You can call me Sandy."

Katrina only nods. She is afraid to reply, but not sure why. Sandy sits down to talk. "I was taking care of your mom here in the hospital, and I had about given up on life. No one knew that though. Your dad came in and started talking; boy, can he talk!"

"Yeah, I know," says Katrina.

"Anyway, he started talking about Jesus and what He means."

"Oh no, my head hurts, and now I have to listen to a nurse preach to me," Katrina interrupts.

"Oh, brother," replies the nurse. "I am *not* preaching. I was telling you about your mom."

"It sounds more like you were talking about you and my dad," says Katrina.

"I think you need more sleep. Please don't say anything to your dad. I don't think he knows who I am. I would like to keep it that way for now," pleads Sandy.

"Okay, I will keep your secret," says Katrina. "Please, let me get some sleep."

Sandy walks out, shaking her head and praying: "God, keep Your hand on that girl. She needs You so badly. I thought I was lost, but You were there for me. Please, help her and her family. I ask all of this, in Jesus's name, amen."

Both men see the nurse walk out, and Chief Tom says out loud, "I wonder if it is safe to go back in the room yet?"

"I don't care; that is my baby in there," states Dale.

As they start to walk back into the room, they hear Katrina on the phone with someone. They look at each other and wonder who she is talking to.

39

Katrina, The Mystery of Prayer

"Hey, do you know why I am in the hospital, Gina?" asks Katrina.

"Yeah, some college guy put something in your drink, and they are trying to frame Eric for it. He swears he didn't do it. He wants me to tell you that he loves you."

Katrina looks up and sees the two men standing by the door and wonders how long they have been there, but continues with her conversation, saying, "I love him too. I have to go, bye!"

"Katrina are you okay?" asks her dad.

"Yes, why didn't you tell me some college guy drugged me? Why is Eric being blamed? I know you don't like him, but he loves me."

Both men look at each other and realize she believes her friend. They know they are fighting a losing battle now.

"There goes the case," mutters Chief Tom. "I will see you later."

"Yeah, bye. Katrina, let's talk," her dad says. "I don't hate Eric. When I called Tom, I had a weird feeling something was wrong with you."

"You mean like psychics do?" asks Katrina.

"No, like the Holy Spirit," says her dad.

"Please, no more preaching. I can only take so much. Let me get some sleep," states Katrina.

"I am going to go see your mom while you sleep. It seems you don't need me here anyway. I will be back later. I *do* love you," her dad says sadly, feeling total despair.

"Fine. Tell her I – I love her," says Katrina.

"I will, baby; get some rest."

Chapter 9

He gives Katrina a kiss on the cheek and hugs her. He never sees the tears coming down her face as he walks out the door. He never realizes how much she needs him right now. The pain is so bad, but not from her head. It is in her heart. She feels like a frightened little girl. "When will the nightmare end?" she thinks, as she cries herself to sleep.

Chapter 10

Dale gets to the nursing home and visits Peggy most of the afternoon.

"Well, Peg, our little girl got by with the skin of her teeth. Some boy nearly raped her. She won't believe it because she loves him. God kept her safe. She is in the hospital right now," he says, looking at his wife, who looks like she is crying.

Dale thinks, *I know what the doctors say, but looking at her, I don't know how much they know.*

"Peggy, please don't cry. She is okay. I am ready for you to come home. Please, wake up," he cries.

"God, thank you for keeping Your hand on Katrina. Give Dale peace. I love you and know you are the answer. Please let Katrina see that soon."

The angel appears and tells Peggy, "The time is coming sooner than you realize. She will know when it is her time."

"What do you mean? Am I going to lose my daughter? Please tell me?" cries Peggy.

"It is in God's hands, like you said."

"What do you mean? Am I going to lose my daughter? Please, please, tell me no," begs Peggy.

As the angel leaves, all Peggy can hear is the angel say, "It is in God's hands, like you said."

Katrina, The Mystery of Prayer

"God, Your Word says that if we pray and believe, all things are possible. I believe You will not let my daughter spend eternity in hell. I believe Your Son died on a cross and rose again. He died for me, but He also died for my daughter. Jesus, help her now. Send angels to protect her. I ask this in Jesus's name, amen."

Dale has fallen asleep while talking to Peggy and holding her hand. As he gets up to leave, he notices her fingers moving. "Peggy, I believe you will be home one day soon," he says as he leaves.

Katrina wakes up as the doctor comes in to see her. He doesn't say much, but he never does. "Katrina, your blood pressure is still low. I want to keep you here another night. It is simply a precaution. Do you understand?"

"Yeah, whatever," she says.

"Are you hurting anywhere?"

"Just my head," Katrina replies weakly.

"I know, that will take time. You were really lucky the other night."

"I know. Everyone keeps telling me," Katrina whines.

"I am leaving. Is there anything you need?" asks the doctor.

The only answer he receives is silence. Katrina rolls over, looks out the window, and wonders, "Why is everyone saying these things about Eric? They don't even know him."

Dale stops and checks on Jarod. They have decided to let him stay with Brother Mike's family while Katrina recovers. Dale arrives at the hospital. Katrina is so happy to see her dad back, but she would never let him know it.

44

Chapter 10

"Katrina, I know this must be confusing, but I am here for you."

"Dad, how was mom? I wish she was here with me," Katrina states.

"I know, me too. We just have to keep praying," says her dad.

"Dad, why does everybody keep saying 'pray?' Everybody has been praying, but Mom still hasn't woken up yet. She may never wake up," Katrina says.

"Don't say that. I never want to hear you say something like that again. God has never let me down. I know things come in His time, not ours. If He wanted your mom, she would already have been taken home. He has His reasons and I trust Him with all my heart. I am not saying everything will always be easy. He never promised us an easy life. He merely promised us life."

"Yeah, where is Mom's life right now?" Katrina asks, crying.

"She has her life. It may not be what we would want for her, but she still *has* it. Even if God took her home right now, she would have life. She would be in Heaven, where she would feel no pain or anything bad. Right now, I can't say she doesn't feel pain. So, He has His reasons for her to be here, and it is not her time to go," says Dale.

"Okay, but I have my reasons for not believing in Him. Mom believed with all her heart and look where it got her."

"Kat, it won't always be that way."

"Daddy, I am tired. Please stay with me."

"I will *always* stay, as long as you want. I love you!"

Katrina, The Mystery of Prayer

Dale and Katrina never see the angel watching over the two of them as they both settle down to rest.

"God, I can't help feeling like I am fighting a losing battle. Why will she not call on Jesus, Your Son. We have taught her Your ways. Lord, please help me with her!" he cries.

It has been a long day, and everyone is exhausted. The nurse stops in and sees that everyone is asleep. She leaves and says a silent prayer for the girl and her family.

Dale wakes up as the nurse shuts the door. He thinks that she looks so familiar but can't remember where he met her. It is really bothering him. *Oh well, I'll figure it out later*, he thinks.

Chapter 11

The next morning is a bright and beautiful day. Katrina's color looks better, and she is smiling. "Hi, Daddy! Can we go home?"

"We have to wait for the doctor to release you."

"Okay," she says, frowning.

The nurse walks in and her dad doesn't waste any time asking her if he knows her. "Do I know you?"

"Yes and no," she replies, smiling.

"Okay, what does that mean?" Dale asks.

"I am Sandy. I took care of your wife when she was in the hospital."

"I remember you now. Did you ever go to that church?" he asks.

"Yes, and thank God that I did. I know what you mean now!" Sandy says.

"I am glad to hear it. You'll have to tell us about it sometime," says Dale.

"I would like to, but the doctor says Katrina can go home today. How is your wife?"

"My wife is the same. Thank you again for taking care of my family," Dale answers.

"No thanks needed. You deserve a thank you though. You don't have any idea how much I think of your family. Well, I have to go. See you later, Katrina. Be well."

Katrina, The Mystery of Prayer

"Bye, Sandy," says Katrina, in an angelic tone.

Dale looks at the two of them and wonders why his daughter is acting like an adult. This is new. He guesses she is growing up. They drive home and he starts thinking about Peggy, and what Katrina has said earlier.

Dale thinks, *Peggy hasn't even seen the house we live in now. How would she like it? The kids seem to have adjusted. It sure is hard raising them. They have a mother, but they don't either. It is like losing a parent to death or divorce. God will look out for them. I am sure of that.*

Katrina calls Gina as soon as she gets home. "Gina, hey, how is everyone?"

"If you mean Eric, he is waiting for you to call."

"I wasn't sure if he would want me to. Does he know it was my dad who called the police?"

"Yeah, he knows, but he figures your dad had a right," replies Gina.

"I am glad he doesn't blame or hate me."

"He blames himself for what happened."

"But, he didn't do anything. It was some college guy. Since they don't know who drugged me, the case has been dropped. How was the party? I don't remember much," says Katrina, with uncertainty.

"They took you out in an ambulance. The police broke up the party. My dad told them kids will be kids, then he yelled at me. When can you leave the house?"

"I'm not grounded, I think. Dad is too worried about me to do that. Why don't you come over? It will be okay with my dad. He forgives everyone. He says he has to because of Jesus's forgiving; you know his beliefs."

"Oh boy, your parents really take this religious stuff serious," Gina states smugly.

Chapter 11

"Yeah, they believe prayer is the answer to everything. I have told my dad it doesn't work. Mom is *still* in a coma," Katrina says weakly, feeling despair.

"Will she ever get to come home, Katrina?"

"Well, she will, *if* she wakes up. Hey, I have to go, but let's get together later."

"Okay, bye!"

Dale overhears his daughter talking. He thinks, *If she would just give Jesus a chance. Why doesn't she believe? He has gotten me through so much. Why can't she see? He is the only reason I can go on without Peggy by my side.*

"God, please do something for Katrina. I ask this, in Jesus's name. Amen."

He has no idea what he is asking from God. God is going to allow something to happen. Dale has to hold onto his faith.

Jarod comes running up the porch, yelling, "I'm home. Is anyone here?"

"Jarod, I'm upstairs with Katrina," replies his dad.

"How is the runaway?" Jarod asks.

"I didn't run away," Katrina cries.

"Oh yeah, last time I checked, you left without permission. That would be considered running away."

"I went to a party. Big deal."

Their dad interrupts, "Katrina and Jarod, enough! It *is* a big deal. Do you realize what could have happened to you?"

"I know; nobody will let me forget it," she yells.

"No! I won't let you forget it," Dad says, crossing his arms. "You are grounded. I just wanted to make sure you were okay. Now that you are, it's time for your

49

Katrina, The Mystery of Prayer

punishment. You can go to school, home, and church. Nowhere else."

"How long does this last?" she cries.

"One month, maybe longer, for you to think about all of this," her dad answers.

"Daddy, please?"

"No! Get some rest now. I will see you in the morning. Jarod, it is time we all went to bed. Goodnight."

"I want to talk to Katrina, if that is, okay?" Jarod asks.

Dale pauses, then sighs. "Okay, but only for a little bit."

"Katrina, what is going on?" asks Jarod. "You used to listen to Mom and Dad. What is happening?"

"Mom is gone, and now I feel like I am losing everyone," she says.

"Mom is not gone! She is sleeping," Jarod yells.

"Yeah, you believe that? God took her from us. Have you seen her lately? She is a vegetable."

"Why are you so mean?" Jarod asks. "God loves her, and He loves us too!"

"Yeah, yeah, I hear you. Look, I need to get some sleep."

"Katrina, I don't want to lose you too. Mom will come home someday. You just watch," he says.

"Goodnight, Jarod."

Meanwhile, Peggy wonders when her family is going to visit again. She needs to hear their voices. Days go by, then weeks. Still, her family doesn't come and see her.

"Have they forgotten me?" she asks the angel by her side.

"No!" the angel says firmly.

Chapter 11

"But, they don't come anymore," she says.

"They pray for you every day. They are living their lives. Dale cries every night for you, but he has to work too. No one has forgotten you."

Peggy asks, "When will this be over?"

"You know it is in God's time. Why do you keep asking?" the angel asks.

"I feel so alone. How is Jarod and Katrina?"

Peggy prays: "God, please help my family. I pray that if there is anyone who doesn't know You as their Lord and Savior, they will accept You today. Please be with Katrina. Lord, help her see Your ways. You are everything to me. Even if I never come out of this, I know you are with me. I pray that someday I will see my family again. In Jesus's name, I pray. Amen."

"Amen," agrees the angel.

Chapter 12

Months go by and Katrina gets better, but she still hasn't accepted Christ. She keeps seeing Eric in secret. Eric wishes they could tell her dad, because after the party something miraculous happened. Eric accepted Jesus as his Lord and Savior. Katrina doesn't understand it at all. They get into his car and decide to go see a movie.

"Katrina, when are you going to talk to your dad about us?" asks Eric.

"I'm not. He forgives everyone, but he still blames you," she says.

"Kat, there is something we need to talk about. This is hard. I understand how your dad feels."

"But you did not do anything wrong!" interrupts Katrina.

"Just listen, I need you to forgive me."

"Oh no, not you too! I have a feeling a sermon is coming on."

"Kat!" Eric yells.

"Okay, go ahead," she replies.

"I need you to forgive me. The college boys gave me the drug, and then I gave it to you."

"Why?" asks Katrina.

Katrina, The Mystery of Prayer

"I thought it was the only way to have you. I didn't stop and think. All I could think about was sex and you wanted to wait."

"I thought you understood."

"I do now," Eric says.

"I forgive you. I know it is hard. I still have feelings for you, but I feel like we should wait," states Katrina.

"Me too! I want us to wait. Ever since I accepted Jesus, something has changed. I am not saying I don't want to. The feelings are still there, but I just want to do what is right," Eric states firmly.

"Okay, so you want me to talk to my dad?" Katrina asks.

"No, I want *us* to talk to your dad."

"Let's just go and see him now and get this over with. He is home if you really want to do this."

"I do," says Eric, "because I love you." He does not know these are his last words to Katrina.

They pull out of the movie theater parking lot, just as a drunk driver crosses the line. Eric never knows what hits him, it happens so quickly. He goes to be with His Lord and Savior, Jesus Christ. Katrina feels a burning in her legs and then nothing. When she wakes up, she is in the hospital again. People are trying to reach her dad, but he is visiting Peggy, and there is no cellphone.

"Why aren't you here, Daddy?" she cries.

Dale turns his radio on in time to hear the news. "Two local teenagers, Eric Jenkins, and Katrina Casteel have been in a car accident. If anyone can reach the family, please have them call the Latham Police

Chapter 12

Department, or go to New Hope Memorial Hospital," says the announcer.

"Oh, my God, please keep her safe. God, I don't know what to do, but I trust You. Katrina needs You. Please, let her be okay, in Jesus's name, amen.

Dale pulls into the hospital, as a hearse is pulling away. He begins to cry. He has never felt as much anguish as he does at this very moment.

"God, I see how much pain you felt when Jesus died. Please, oh please, don't let it be my baby. She is everything to me. Your Son died for her too. Please, oh please, in Jesus's name, amen," he prays.

He opens his door, and Chief Tom yells,. "Dale, are you okay?"

"Katrina?"

"She is alive," states Chief Tom.

"Thank you, God," he cries, and falls to his knees.

Chief Tom helps him up and tells him what happened, according to eye-witnesses. "Katrina is awake and calling for her dad," he tells him.

They walk to her room in silence. As they go into the room, the doctor walks out. "Mr. Casteel, we need to talk," Dr. Brown states.

"Can I see my daughter first?" asks Dale.

"Let's talk first, and then you can see her. Chief Tom, can you wait with Katrina?"

"Yes," he replies, and walks into the room.

"Dale, she was in a bad wreck. The boy she was with died instantly. His name is Eric. I don't know what she remembers, but she keeps asking about him. I think it would be best if you told her. Katrina has some swelling around the spinal cord. I don't think it is permanent,

Katrina, The Mystery of Prayer

but I cannot promise you anything at this time. She is paralyzed for now," says Dr. Brown.

Dale cannot believe what he is hearing. This has to be a nightmare, first Peggy, and now Katrina. "Dr. Brown is there anything else I need to know?" he asks.

"Not really; she is bruised and cut up pretty bad, but those should heal okay. I am worried about her emotional state at this time though."

"Please, let me see my daughter."

"I will check on her tomorrow. Go ahead and see her," says Dr. Brown.

Dale slowly pushes the door open. He is not ready for what he sees. Katrina is asleep, but she looks so broken. The left side of her face is bruised. Her forehead has a bandage on it, but the right side looks fine. He walks over to her, taking her hand.

"Kat," he cries, tears rolling down his face. "I am here. Baby, I am so happy you are alive."

"Daddy," she moans, "how is Eric?"

"Let's talk later; right now, you need to rest," he says, sitting on the side of her bed, in fear of hurting her more.

"I can't feel my legs!" she cries as she falls asleep."

"Tom, do you know anything about this Eric boy?" Dale whispers to the chief of police, who is sitting in the chair quietly.

"Yes, I do. He started going to church after the party. Dale, he accepted Jesus as his Lord and Savior. He was a totally different kid. I don't know why this happened, but he could have been the answer to your prayers for Katrina. She listened to him when she wouldn't listen to anyone else."

Chapter 12

"I am glad to know he is in Heaven. It makes it a little easier knowing that. The problem will be telling Kat. She still blames God for her mother, and now this," Dale says wearily.

"I don't know what to say or do except pray. Is there anyone you want to call?" asks Chief Tom, who has been a dear friend of the family.

"Yes, my preacher, and the prayer line. I need someone to be there for Jarod. I have to be here for Katrina," replies Dale sadly.

"He can stay with Charity and me. She will be glad to watch him. You know she likes mothering everyone."

"Are you sure?" Dale asks. "I keep asking for help lately."

"I am sure it is time for people to help you. Think about how many times Peggy kept someone at your house. No one can do it alone. Sometimes, you have to ask for help. Hey, we are *all* children of God. I am only his servant."

"Thank you, and God bless you," Dale says weakly.

Chapter 13

Katrina wakes up early the next morning. The first thing she sees is her dad. "Daddy, can we talk?" she asks.

"Yes, what do you want to talk about?" he asks hesitantly.

"I want to know how Eric is doing?" she questions.

There is a silence as Dale pauses. "Kat, I am sorry."

"No! Oh, please no! He can't be? I love him," Katrina cries.

"Lean over here," her dad says.

She leans over and cries while her dad holds her in his arms. "I realize this must be hard."

"Daddy, we were coming to see you," she cries. "He wanted to apologize. Ever since he started going to church, something changed in him."

"What do you mean?" he asks.

"He accepted Jesus, and now he is dead. He wanted to talk with you. If I had said no, he would still be alive."

"Kat, don't do this to yourself. I heard he accepted Jesus as his personal Lord and Savior. Right now, he is with Jesus in Heaven."

"How can you be so sure? Look at Mom. God is so mean," she says with conviction.

Katrina, The Mystery of Prayer

"Kat, our God is a *loving* God. Look at what His Son went through for our sins. Do you think it was easy for Him to watch His Son die? I hurt so badly when I thought you were dead. You do know fathers hurt too, right?" Dale asks.

"Daddy, if He loves me so much, why is He letting these things happen?" Katrina asks.

"It isn't about you, baby, it is about Jesus."

"Eric is dead because of Him!"

"No, Kat, he is *alive* because of Him. We will have to wait until we get to Heaven to see Him though," says her dad.

"I don't understand," she cries. "It seems like all I do since Mom's accident is cry."

"I know, and I keep praying you will understand one day soon."

Katrina changes the subject. "Will I ever walk again?"

"The doctor said he believes you will, but he could not make any promises."

"Daddy, can I go to Eric's funeral?" Katrina asks but is afraid of the answer.

"I don't know. It depends on what the doctor says," he replies. "Get some rest."

"Okay," Katrina says. "My head hurts."

"Kat, can we pray?"

"Dad, *you* can, but I'm still having a hard time. Eric accepted Him, so that must mean something, but look where he is now. I just don't know."

"Please let Jesus into your heart," he says. "I will pray for both of us and Eric's family." Dale continues, "God, forgive me. Help me where I fall short. Please be with Eric's family. Watch over them and give them

Chapter 13

peace. If they don't know You as their Lord and Savior, I pray they will soon. Be with Katrina, and help her heal, physically and spiritually. Give her Your peace. I pray that You will watch over Jarod and Peggy too. I ask this, in Jesus's name, amen."

Katrina turns her head away so her dad cannot see her crying. It seems as if she is losing her whole world: Mom, and now Eric. *She wonders, who is next? Why is God punishing me? I am not even sure if He is real.* She is thinking all these things and more as she falls asleep.

Brother Mike and people from the church come by and visit Katrina. The ladies' class feels they should help with Katrina. Dale can't be at the hospital all the time, and Katrina needs spiritual guidance. Peggy's best friend, Sue, begins to stay with Katrina most days while her kids are in school.

Physical therapy is harder than Katrina realized. It hurts, but she still can't make her legs move like she wants. Nurses, doctors, family, and friends encourage her. Soon, she is ready to talk to someone, and Sue is there.

"Sue, I need to know something," Katrina says.

"Go ahead, ask away. If I can answer you, I will," Sue replies.

"How do you *know* Jesus is real?"

"I know because I believe in the Word of God, the Bible."

"Yea, but how do you *know* it is true?"

"God's Word is the only thing that is completely true. I have faith in God," says Sue, with confusion about this conversation.

"But *how?*" asks Katrina frustrated.

Katrina, The Mystery of Prayer

"Katrina, let me ask you some questions. Who is your mother?"

"Peggy Casteel."

"Are you sure?"

"Yes, I am sure!" Katrina says defensively.

"But *how*?" Sue says, feeling more secure in this conversation.

"She gave me life. She carried me for nine months."

"So, you have complete faith that she is your mother?" she asks.

"Yes!" Katrina says sternly.

"Like you have faith in her, I have *more* faith in God. Years from now, people could question who your mother is right?"

"Yes, I guess so."

"If they didn't know her personally, that does not change who your mom is though. They just don't have faith in what they read or heard. I *know* Jesus is the Son of God. The Bible is a history book. It is the only history book that tells us about the past and the future. Cool, huh?"

"Okay, I'm listening," Katrina says.

"Just because some people don't believe, it doesn't make them right. Jesus died. No one can deny that. They deny He is the Son of God. Close your eyes."

Katrina listens and closes her eyes.

"Okay, imagine yourself with Jesus," Sue continues. "A man walks up and asks, 'If one of you has to die, who will it be?' Jesus already did that for you at Calvary so you could live. Can you imagine the pain He felt on the Cross? He loves you *that* much. He loves you more than your parents ever could. Don't ever doubt the love of

Chapter 13

Christ. He died so you could live. Someday, you will see Eric again in Heaven."

"Sue, I want my mom," Katrina says.

"I know; we all miss her. I do believe she will wake up though. The Holy Spirit keeps laying you and her on my heart. God has a plan. Go visit her soon."

"I have to get out of here first," Katrina says.

"Work on getting well."

"Thanks, Sue."

"Thanks for what?"

"You being here; it helps. Sometimes, I feel so lonely. I miss Mom. I never realized how much she meant to me until she was gone."

"She will be back. Have faith in God."

"I'm trying, but it is hard."

"Katrina, Satan is not going to make it easy for you. He hates you as much as Jesus loves you."

"I haven't done anything for him to hate me."

"Girl, for someone raised in church, you really don't know much. It is his *job* to steal, kill, and destroy. People keep praying for you. He wants to see you in Hell, not Heaven. He cannot control anything in Heaven, but Hell is his. It is kind of like a custody battle, you could say. God wants you to accept His Son, Jesus, as Your Lord and Savior, so you can be with Him in Heaven. Satan wants to keep you from doing that so he can have you in Hell. Sorry for being so blunt, but is seems like someone needs to be."

"Sue, you've been a big help," Katrina says, starting to get up. "Thanks, I have to go to therapy now."

Chapter 14

Katrina feels like there is something going on within her. Something is different or weird; she is not sure. It is the same daily routine, but she doesn't understand the need that keeps growing in her to talk to other people. She has heard all of this before now, but it didn't make sense then.

"God, I'm still not sure," she whispers quietly.

Later, back in her room, the doctor stops to visit.

"Katrina and Mr. Casteel, I'm going to let Katrina go home late this afternoon. She is making some improvements, but it will take time. She needs to come back three days a week for physical therapy. The nurse will show you some exercises you can do at home," says the doctor.

"Thank you, Dr. Brown. May God bless you," Dale replies.

Sandy, the nurse, comes in later to show her the exercises. She is smiling from ear-to-ear. She knows something great is about to happen. She doesn't know when or where, but knows it is coming soon.

"Hi, Katrina," says Sandy.

"Hi. Did you come to talk?" asks Katrina.

"No, but we can talk. Hi, Dale."

"Hi, nice to see you again," Dale answers back.

Katrina, The Mystery of Prayer

"What did you want to talk about, Katrina?" asks Sandy.

"Well, you tried to tell me about my parents, and how they affected your life."

"Yes," answers Sandy.

"I am ready to listen."

"Okay, but I want to know if it would be okay if we pray first with you? I can show you some exercises while we talk."

"Sure," replies Katrina.

Dale doesn't know what is coming over his daughter. She seems to be changing right before his eyes. Sandy takes his and Katrina's hands. Katrina looks nervous. Her dad smiles and takes her other hand.

"Our Father in Heaven, hallowed be Your Name, Your Kingdom come, Your will be done, on earth as it is in Heaven. Give us this day, our daily bread. Forgive us our debts, as we also have forgiven our debtors. Lead us not into temptation, but deliver us from the evil one. Amen."

"Okay, Katrina, let's talk," Sandy says, as she begins showing Katrina different leg exercises.

"I met your dad when I was at my worst. There he was, with your mom, and he still believes God was with her and him. I haven't seen such faith since my grandmother. When he came in, I was getting off work soon, and I was planning on killing myself that night," she says.

"But why?" asks Katrina.

"I felt alone and like nobody loved me. I felt like I was simply wasting air. I wanted out. Your dad talked to me through it, but he had no idea."

Chapter 14

"Sandy?" Dale asks.

"Dale, you did what the Holy Spirit asked you to do and thank you for that. I've never forgotten you or your family."

"Thank you, Sandy; you don't know what that means to me," Dale says.

"Hmm…" interrupts Katrina.

"Sorry Katrina, your dad asked me if I knew Jesus as my Lord and Savior. This is what I told him: 'I walked the church aisle, but I always felt the same.'"

"Do you remember what you said Dale?" Sandy asks.

"Yes, I hope that I never feel the same," he replies.

"Yes, and that got me thinking. The more you talked, the more I wanted to cry. I went home, and instead of taking my life, I gave it to God. I accepted Jesus as my Lord and Savior. I agree with you, Dale, I never want to be the same again either."

"Sandy, did it really make that big of a difference?" asks Katrina.

"Yes, Katrina. Try bending your toes now," Sandy says. "I need to check with someone. I'll be right back."

"Is everything okay?" asks Dale.

"Yes, I will be right back," Sandy says, and leaves the room.

She wasn't gone long and came back with the doctor.

"Katrina, try bending your toes," requests the doctor.

Dale watches his daughter bend her toes. It is the best thing he has seen in a long time.

"Thank you, God," Dale cries.

Katrina, The Mystery of Prayer

"Yes, that is true. Katrina, do you feel anything?" the doctor asks.

"No," she replies.

"How about now, Katrina?" the doctor asks, checking her feet.

"It feels like a needle," Katrina says, wincing.

"Good, because it is a pin. It looks like the paralysis is leaving. I noticed some improvement, but this is more than I had expected so soon. I don't know what has happened, but keep it up," Dr. Brown says and leaves the room.

All three of them look at each other. Two of them know what is happening, but one of them is still lost. "Katrina, when you get home, read Psalms 119:41-48 out of your Bible."

"Okay, Dad, can we go see Mom? I haven't seen her in ages," Katrina asks.

"Yes, I would like that," he replies.

Sandy smiles, knowing what is coming: Jesus saved her, and now He is going to do the same for Katrina. She can feel it.

Dale and Katrina drive to the nursing home to see Peggy. They both are quiet. Katrina keeps thinking about what Sandy said, while Dale keeps his eyes on the road and Jesus. Dale walks slowly into the nursing home, pushing Katrina in a wheelchair.

"Dad, can I see Mom alone for a minute?" Katrina asks shyly.

"Yes, baby."

Katrina goes in, rolls up next to her mother, and takes her hand. She starts talking to her.

68

Chapter 14

"Mom, I am sorry for not believing you," she cries. "Eric died. You are here, and I am in a wheelchair. I blamed God."

She notices the Bible on the table. What is it Sandy wants me to read? Oh yeah, Psalms 119:41-48. She looks it up and reads it:

> May Your unfailing love come to me, O LORD. Your Salvation according to Your promise; then I will answer the one who taunts me, for I trust in Your Word. Do not snatch the word of truth from my mouth, for I have put my hopes in Your law, forever and ever. I will walk in freedom, for I have sought out Your precepts. I will speak of Your status before kings and will not be put to Shame for I delight in Your commands because. I love them. I lift up my hands to Your commands, Which I love, and I meditate on Your decrees.

Dale opens the door and hears her reading. He begins to pray. "God, please reach her. Amen," is all he can say.

Katrina turns around and sees him standing behind her. She is crying so hard. He walks over and takes Peggy's hand. He knows it is Katrina's decision. This is one thing she has to decide and do on her own.

"Daddy, please pray with me. I don't know what to do for sure," she says.

"Just admit you are a sinner, and accept Jesus into your heart," her dad tells her.

"But that sounds so easy," she says.

Chapter 15

Peggy can hear her baby. She has to ask God for help again.

"God, please help Katrina. Amen," she says.

The angel appears to her one last time. He says, "It is time."

Katrina cries, as she starts praying, "God, please forgive me. I am a sinner. I have been selfish, and I need You in my life. I accept Jesus as my Lord and Savior. I know He is Your Son. He died for my sins. God, please," she cries. "Forgive me, I am sorry. Help me to be what You want me to be for You. Be with my mom, not for me, but for her. I love you, Jesus. I ask all this in Jesus's name, amen."

"Amen," the three of them say in unison.

Katrina and her dad look at her mom at the same time. She is looking at them and smiling.

"Mom, can you hear me?" Katrina cries.

"Kat, please don't cry."

Peggy sees Dale crying. "Dale, you are not helping right now. Stop crying!" she says.

Dale rings for the nurse to come. He cannot believe he has his wife again. Katrina can't stop crying. God has performed three miracles today. They were small to Him, but everything to her.

Katrina, The Mystery of Prayer

"Thank you, Jesus!" Peggy yells.

Nurses run in and start checking Peggy. It is a miracle. No one can explain what is happening, but the three of them know. There are more tears of happiness.

Peggy says, "Katrina, I am so proud of you."

No one has said that to her in a long time. She has thought she would never hear that again.

"Katrina, let's get better together. I will probably need a wheelchair too."

All Dale can say is, "I love you and thank you, God!"

Peggy laughs with the joy of the Lord.

Three months later, they are in their home. The family is gathering with friends, old and new, for a celebration. There is laughing, crying, singing, praising, and lots of hugs. It is a miracle from God. Sandy has the family standing together for a family picture. Peggy and Katrina stand in front of the door, while Jarod and Dale kneel in front of them. Beside the front door, a picture is posted that reads:

> Except the Lord
> build the house,
> they labor
> in vain that
> build it.

Psalms 127:1

Once again, the family is together.